Political Criticisms & Treatise On Socio-Capitalism Volume II

By: Thomas Glenn

There's always a yearning of memory to remember simpler times when a person was a child. Deep down that is something we must cherish, but yet keep disciplined in an odd way. As you get older and learn things from a larger perspective, you grow both independent and responsible at the same time. With freedom comes responsibility.

I write this second volume to my original work not for political, social, and financial gain but to try and promote intellectual thought and debate within our society. That, as well as to lay down potential blueprints for future politicians and various other civil servants to look into and consider for the betterment of the society within our nation and outside of it. Again, it was not intellectuals who gave me the courage to undertake this task but instead the four classes of people I have come across. Those classes being the farmer, the worker, the soldier, and the scholar.

I also write this piece to gladly and gratefully share my ideals and knowledge with others. Wealth does not just come from your financial standing and the physical material you have. It comes from the knowledge that a person possesses and dedicates their lives towards accumulating for the sake of promoting their own physical and intellectual standing in the world.

There must be a vision of a welfare system that is both public and private. One in which the politicians, bankers, philosophers, laborers, scientists, farmers, and soldiers all come forth to contribute their worth and good to the whole of society. One in which they wish to see it prosper and be preserved in the grand interest of all.

This type of welfare system should be promoted and preserved. It must be more than charity. We should not say to the rich, "Please, give something to the poor." Much rather we should say, "People, help yourselves. Everyone must help." Whether you are rich or poor, one should always strictly hold onto the belief that there is always someone in a worse situation than I am, and I should like to help this person as an equal friend. If one should say, "Yes, but I do have to sacrifice a lot." then that is the glory of giving. When you make sacrifices and contributions for your community then you can walk around with your head held high.

MILITARY POLICY

We need our fighting men and women at home to make us competitive in the industrially economic field, financial sector, farming sector, and educational field. The fighting men and women would not be disbanded from the military though, reason being is that if we were to do so it would cost more to disband them much rather than to keep them in the military. They could easily be reassigned and commissioned to work within the US and abroad, mainly South America, to help with economic reconstruction under the guise of forward engineers and possible advisors to contractors that'd be allowed to operate. Our military is a vital branch of our whole community, and they cannot, nor should not, be forgotten. That way we can more effectively compete with China. Despite the fact they're the second country we owe the most money to, we need to keep heavy tabs on them. Japan is the first country we owe the most money to, but their dreams of controlling a vast empire, The Empire of the Rising Sun, was crushed since we dropped the a-bombs, Fat Man and Little Boy, on them. They produce a lot of our technology with both research & development. That, and they helped us out in the early 80's when we were going through a recession brought on by the Iranian Revolution, which cut our oil supply. That recession was also brought on by some of Jimmy Carter's actions in office. There's also the fact that with near each recession we've had since the 80's that they've bought bonds to certain companies and public services within our country to help keep them afloat.

MIDDLE EASTERN & ISRAELI POLICY

The issues of the Middle East are a sensitive and fragile area of social politics due to differing religious ideologies. The Abrahamic religions Judaism, Christianity, and Islam hold a strong sway within the regions of the Middle East, but it is mainly Islam that holds the strongest influence due to it being heavily practiced and promoted by the Ottoman Empire and the preceding Islamic empires and countries that emerged before it in the region shortly after 610 AD. Islam was founded and started by Muhammad, who became the first prophet of that religion. He started that religion in 610 AD shortly after supposedly entering a cave and hearing their version of the Lord God's, Allah's, voice as well as being visited by the Archangel Gabriel. That religion sprung from and was heavily influenced by Judaism, Christianity, and a bit of Hinduism. Both Christianity and Islam sprung from Judaism, splitting away from it due to differing religious doctrines & ideologies that were taken too literally. Christianity came to be due to the doctrines and teachings of Jesus Christ that strayed away from the normal Jewish teachings at that time, his arrest and crucifixion at the hands of the Romans, Jews, and Philistines. His disciples and their collective followers viewed him as the Jewish Messiah, son of God, God incarnate, and a martyr for being ultimately persecuted and killed for his beliefs.

From my perspective they're all just children playing with primitive concepts and toys because they've been subjected to it for centuries and millennias. Tradition can be hard to get rid of. I agree that we should withdraw from there and let them fight it out on their own, but we cannot entirely permit such a thing to transpire for the gravest and most horrifying war crimes and crimes against humanity can be committed by both sides of the fence. The issue of sacred land to both the Judaic and Islamic people's within Israel, the former state of Palestine, is one of the other things that is driving the Isaeli-Palestinian Conflict. The US and its allies throughout the past century have made establishing Israel, the home for the Jews, their ultimate crusade within the region. That social political endeavor was even more so imposed after the events of WWII and the Holocaust to help protect the Jewish population and to make them feel that they had a land they could call home. However, the Jews were originally from the Middle Eastern region to begin with since they migrated from there to Egypt becoming a conscripted military force and then a conscripted work force under Pharaoh Ramses II of Egypt. Moses, one of the original prophets of God, then defied the Pharaoh's rule and had his people launch a mass exodus out of Egypt to the east in the hopes of finding their Promised Land. That Promised Land, after venturing through the desert for forty years, was the regions of what is today currently Israel and the former state of Palestine. There are numerous other factors though that fuel into the conflict.

I digress, now, with returning to the original topic of the Israeli-Palestinian Conflict, their lands should be ultimately divided. The various lands of which the citizens of the former Palestinian state want should be taken into consideration and honored. Those Palestinians along the Gaza Strip and throughout Israel that wish to secede from the Jewish state should be permitted to do so, so long as they lay down their arms and negotiate diplomatic talks with the representatives of the Israeli government.

Our attention should be pulled from the Middle East, but not entirely. We could still have three advisors, six CIA agents, twelve Secret Service agents, and twenty one private security members attached to those nations. Each American advisor can have two CIA agents, four Secret Service agents, and seven private security team members assigned to them to help with gathering information, negotiate treaties, and see that those nations do not impose their religious ideologies on other countries. The Middle East could easily trade with African countries if they all had a single powerful central bank and central currency to trade with the Middle Eastern countries.

Iran and Afghanistan should be collectively isolated by the whole international community in my opinion. Such theocratic states are absurd and outdated. They shouldn't be tolerated, nor given any weight in political and business decisions. Let them feel the full weight of unified world sanctions out on them and let's see their people starve to the point of inward rebellion. We shouldn't even be trying to impose democracy on them. The Arabs and Islamic people there only understand one thing, brute force.

Individual native dictators loyal and determined to maintain peace in the region should be put into power.

With oil the US should lessen its restrictions and sanctions on Venezuela as well as other South American countries, come together on a political and economic basis to potentially build a series of pipelines with numerous backup valves in place to prevent a catastrophic breach. It'd not only be good for their countries but ours as well. We wouldn't have to heavily rely on Saudi Arabia and other Middle Eastern countries for oil. I say we should just pull out and let them solve their own mess to a degree, but have the various agents previously mentioned attempt to produce peace talks that'll benefit almost all parties involved. A lot of the problems in the Middle East right now stem from the Sykes-Picot Agreement of WWI and the collective international western nations trying to hold true to that agreement, the Grand Mufti's (Islamic Pope) attempt to oust the British from the region during WWII with limited German aid, the Jews being granted Palestinian land, the Iranian Revolution, and the Soviet-Afghan War. It was mainly the Sykes-Picot agreement though because it divided the Ottoman Empire into the countries we know of in the region today.

AFRICAN CONTINENT POLICY

With the African Continent we, the western and even eastern international community, should permit and aid the various African countries with establishing a central bank. That bank should initially and temporarily distribute interest free and debt free bills to help with reconstructing the infrastructures and economies of those nations. After those nations have been reconstructed, living standards have improved, and their economies become stable those bills should be retired and replaced by interest bearing bills.

The whole global community should also aid with the construction of an oil pipeline system within their various countries. That pipeline system should link up with the Saudi Arabian and other Middle Eastern countries to make both the Middle East & Africa prosperous. Our own advisors with the CIA, Secret Service, and private military personnel assigned to them should help with smoothing the transition of diverting the Middle East's resources to

Africa and vice versa. The Middle Eastern countries though should not impose and try to promote their religious ideologies and practices on the African countries. There should be a treaty that both prohibits and enforces that in the effort of preserving peace in Africa. Also, US military engineers and companies should invest their time into helping those African economies, public projects, and private projects that seek to find alternative forms of renewable energy to have the African Continent have self sustaining energy. Mass irrigation and farming projects should be attempted within North Africa to try and help feed the ever growing population of that continent. The US and other nations should distribute food to them through both public and private trade during the time they try to perfect a mass farming system.

Now, there are certain parts of Africa that are unfortunately locked in states of civil war, infighting, and mass poverty. The various African states that are locked in civil war and infighting should be approached diplomatically by the combined efforts of our advisors and reasonably compliant Middle Eastern and Russian ones as well. If the conflicts can be resolved through diplomatic means then that will be a true accomplishment. However, should tensions be further stirred and diplomacy falls apart due to the native country's conflicting parties involved to reach a compromise, then the international community should endeavor unanimously to replace those parties with a compliant native regime that appeals to all the international parties involved.

SOUTH AMERICAN & IMMIGRATION POLICY

A portion of the US's current illegal immigration problems could be solved if we focused on promoting and enforcing friendly relations with the South American countries. If we did so and helped those other countries; such as Mexico, Columbia, Nicaragua, Venezuela, Chile, and the numerous other South American nations; promote their economies and standards of living, then there would most likely be a reduction of immigrants, mainly illegals, flooding into the US from those regions. The situation with the advisors and the government as well as private agents assigned to them could easily be put into place in the South American countries with the embassies we have there, too.

The situation of possibly linking the Keystone Pipeline, and various other oil pipelines already currently existing in South America, again, could easily be solved for the US by opening up Venezuela and other South American countries to us with reducing their sanctions and bringing them to the negotiating table to both promote our economies as well as to build a vast oil pipeline system with the US being the beating heart of it. Various Army and other military branch engineers could be reassigned and commissioned to aid in the construction. They'd still be part of the US military under the guise of forward engineers that'd work with various contractors to help set the extensive pipeline system up.

In regards to illegal immigration, the Border Patrol, DEA, and FBI should work in tandem with special forces units under military jurisdiction to heavily and aggressively hunt down various Cartels that traffic drugs and humans into as well as out of the US. There should be multiple bases spread out along the border in accordance with the number of districts each bordering US state has. That type of action could be seen as an act of aggression and prelude to war with army buildup. Despite that fact, we have a border to regularly patrol, inspect, and protect to prevent anyone from potentially abusing and exploiting the populations located around there. We cannot permit mass lawlessness on our southern border. The option of doing this would be costly, but it's a better and more inexpensive alternative from building a border wall that'd be more damaging to the environment. Plus, the Cartels could easily tunnel underneath it. It'd be like the Vietcong & North Vietnamese Army in a way with smuggling drugs, humans, and guns throughout the region. All except the vast tunnel system they'd use would be on our own damn border.

The various South American Cartels in power and operating down there are more reactionary since we've imposed sanctions on their countries for the sake of containment on both socialism and communism. The Cartels operate outside the official government jurisdiction, allowing corruption to happen so they can both profit from it as well as provide goods and services to those countries. Kind of like how the Italian Mob was before Mussolini came to power. Any assistance that the South American governments need with ousting the Cartels or at least appealing to some of their demands should be taken into consideration. In many ways some of the Cartels represent the disenfranchised and impoverished within those nations. They exist as a quasi-nation and paramilitary force in some regards that help maintain a certain degree of order within some of those nations.

Immigration Customs & Enforcement, otherwise known as ICE, could potentially help with housing any illegals that come across our border. They'd need to treat those people humanely though and not like cattle or concentration camp inmates. There's being passionate about protecting our border, which we should do, and then there's being compassionately considerate in regards to treating them like human beings. The illegals should be deported back where they came from.

GOVERNMENT CONTRACTING

In regards to government contract, especially with research and development, companies should be able to compete for them with limited subsidies from the government while receiving tax cuts for doing so, so they can put the money up front for it. The companies that are the more favorable and present better, more efficient technologies such as vehicles, weapons, spacecrafts, and other advanced materials that can produce cheap renewable energy will be chosen to carry out the contracts. China, despite being one of our biggest manufacturing countries due to Richard Nixon opening them up to us economically, should be heavily monitored since they're communists. Communism crushes the individual liberties and civil rights of its citizens, making them mere slaves in a way to an ever abusive economic as well as political system. Thing is though, China permits rudimentary free markets within its borders to promote their economy and some of the livelihood of its citizens so long as they behave and do not criticize the communist government.

That money of which the competing companies save could be put to good use with both promoting their businesses and investing it in new technologies such as small plasma based shields for the troops on the battlefield or finding new alternatives to generate adequate self sustaining energy. Companies would no longer distribute goods to the military at a higher rate than what their actual market value is. There's profits and then there's just strong arm, extortionist lobbying. Lobbyists need to be taken out of the picture, too. A lobbyist is just a middleman between you and getting a good service. Kind of like a weather man sending an intern outside to check the actual weather before he makes his prediction.

The CEOs of the various social media companies should work in tandem with the FBI and CIA, making sure there are no religious zealots and dissenters that impose their beliefs on others within our nation as well as outside.

NASA, despite being crucial to our endeavor of potentially perfecting interplanetary as well as intergalactic space travel, should be privatized and not have so many restrictions put on them. Elon Musk's SpaceX should work with them in the effort of helping to perfect space travel as well as terraforming planets. Let's face it, there's 8 billion of us on this planet and there's starting to get to be very little room.

FEDERAL RESERVE AUDITING

Certain people, mainly Libertarians, have always brought up the concept of auditing the Federal Reserve Bank, otherwise known as the central bank of the United States. It would not entirely be unwise to do so since it exists as its own separate entity outside of strict government regulation and control. It's its own private financial institution. It conducts financial and even some investment business both inside the US and overseas in various other countries. It is that way for a good reason to help prevent it from being widely misused and exploited for personal political gain. It does help with keeping both the economy and American dollar's value at a relatively stable point without it going through rapid inflation. However, auditing it is not completely out of the question since again it is its own financial institution.

Many others, outside the Libertarian way of thinking, consider auditing the Federal Reserve to be unwise since it'd be more damaging to the US dollar's value and economy. There's no doubt that it'd be damaging, but only to a degree and on a small level if it's handled properly and effectively. With auditing the Federal Reserve you could easily have the Department of Justice and the Internal Revenue Service through the Treasury Department do it. It would be an exhausting and prolonged process, no doubt. Certain large executive businesses and industries would, yes, be impacted, but not so much if certain bills were commissioned and distributed by the government through the Department of Treasury to those said businesses. Those bills should be interest free and debt free forms of credit that give those businesses the ability to help keep their businesses afloat as well as to promote their works. Those pre-approved bills from the Senate and House of Representatives could cover those businesses while the Federal Reserve Bank is being audited. Any finances that are then reclaimed and taken from the Federal Reserve through the auditing process could also help fund those bills alongside tax payer money to prevent the American public from being fully forced to fund them in the long run. Those bills should have a time stamp on them as well determining how long they are good for until they're called back for repayment. Those bills should be limited and not given out in excess though to prevent an economic bubble that could potentially pop and lead to a grave economic depression as well as recession. The further excess amount that could be pulled from the auditing process should also be used to help pay down the US's national debt. After the Federal Reserve has been fully audited by the DOJ and the IRS through the various committees they put together, they will be permitted to remain as an independent agency outside of government jurisdiction with some restrictions with the various laws that could be put into place during the auditing process. The interest free bills when they meet their expiration date can then be revoked to appease the private bankers of the Federal Reserve as well as to make them feel that they still have a crucial role in our society. The Federal Reserve also helps to manage our debt, and going completely out of debt is not entirely the wisest thing to do at times for our credit rates may plummet should we pay off the national debt in full and be in a prolonged period of no debt.

Should certain small and large companies feel uncertain about possibly having the Treasury Department interest free bills be distributed to them, then they can produce bonds that the everyday American citizen or various other companies within the US can buy. Those bonds can be subject to compound interest as well as inflation, which we all pray does not entirely happen in regards to inflation with such economic action of auditing the Federal Reserve. That way those companies can still stay relatively intact as well as help benefit either the everyday American citizen or other companies. With those bonds they should strictly be purchased by various companies, agencies, and individuals within our borders. We should no longer have foreign countries, such as Japan & China, purchase them because then our debt will greatly increase again. Yes, those foreign countries and others pay for them, but they wait and hold onto them for a prolonged period of time until they can just smack them down on the table when it reaches a high enough maturity and we'd owe them compound interest plus inflation.

DIFFERENT CENTRAL BANKING HISTORY

BRITISH EMPIRE

The British Empire has heavily relied upon the Bank of England, which was established in 1694 and allowed the national banking system within the British Empire to be privatized. They heavily imposed interest rates upon the various currencies that they issued to have a positive return on various investments and bids. Many of the central banks throughout the world, including the Federal Reserve Bank of the United States, have modeled themselves and their institutions after them.

RUSSIAN EMPIRE

The Russian Empire before WWI was trying to establish their own centralized bank that distributed interest free money. That would've greatly helped the Russian peasantry at the time, as well as upset people on Wall

Street along with the Federal Reserve. The Russian Empire also putting together a centralized bank that distributed interest free money would've upset the Bank of England as well. It would've upset the Vatican Bank as well since much of the Russian population at the time was Orthodox, a splinter cell of Christian faith. The Vatican could see that particular Russian Central Bank be an extension of the Orthodox faith, which has almost always been in ideological conflict with the Catholic and even Christian Protestant world.

Interest free money would've made it so the Russian Empire didn't go into severe debt with the concept of usury, conjuring money out of thin air, which would've kept certain businesses in fine standing since they wouldn't have to owe extra money on top of loans they took out. The extra money that a business made without the concept of usury could then be taxed and taken into account to help further promote the Russian central bank and the economy.

The Germans can be ultimately blamed though for the fall of the Russian Empire and the start of the Russian Revolution because they aided Vladimir Lenin with sneaking back into the country via train. They did it though to quickly end the war on the eastern front, so then they could focus their full attention towards the west. Wall Street actually covertly funded and helped the Bolsheviks during the Russian Revolution. They even supplied western engineers, scientists, and capitalist bankers to Joseph Stalin who wanted them to help perfect his workers paradise.

The US even had a stake in the Russian Revolution with supporting both the Reds (Bolsheviks) and the Whites (Czar loyalists) in Russia. Some of our own troops were dispatched to the oil fields in Siberia to help protect them and keep them secure for which ever side won the revolution.

UNITED STATES

During the American Civil War from 1861-1865 President Abraham Lincoln was looking for ways to help fund the Union and its military. He first went to the bankers who were willing to help pay for it, but the interest rate on the loans would be between 24% and 36%. President Lincoln wasn't fond of the idea at all and turned away from that prospect with distress. He and his cabinet then shortly came up with the idea of producing legal tender paper money with no interest rate and no debt value to it. They distributed it through the Treasury Department to help fund the Union, the military, and various public services. In total they distributed over $400 million of these treasury bills & notes throughout the course of the war. The exact number is actually $448,338,902 that they distributed. It did a tremendous job with helping fund the Union's efforts in the war as well as promoting its economy. They called these treasury notes and bills Greenbacks since they were printed in green ink on the back. However, certain international bankers, particularly from the Bank of England, were not entirely fond of Lincoln's actions.

The London Times even printed a statement shortly after the Greenbacks came into circulation. The statement went like this, "If that mischievous financial policy, which had its origin in the North American Republic, should become indurated to a fixture, then that government will furnish its own money without cost. It will pay off debt and be without a debt. It will have all the money necessary to carry out its own commerce. It will become prosperous beyond precedent in the history of civilized governments of the world. The brains and wealth of all countries will go to North America. That government must be destroyed, or it will destroy every monarchy on the globe."

The British government in power at that time wanted to side with and aid the Confederacy to see them become the victors since they still used interest based currency. However, they couldn't entirely do so since the British people genuinely liked Lincoln and were in admiration as well support of his effort to pass the 13th Amendment, otherwise known as the Emancipation Proclamation. That, and the Russian Tsar at the time dispatched Russian naval vessels to the US to be placed under Lincoln's command and disposal.

Shortly after Lincoln was assassinated by John Wilkes Booth in April, 1865 the US government revoked the Greenback currency printed under his presidency. The National Banking Act was soon signed into law as well which allowed national banks to be privatized and the money they distributed to be interest bearing. In 1972 the US Treasury Department was asked to calculate how much the US would have been in debt during the war if Lincoln had gone with the loans with the high interest rates instead of producing his own money. They calculated that he saved them from a $4 billion deficit at that time.

In 1913 the National Banking Act was replaced by the Federal Reserve Act implemented by President Woodrow Wilson when he forced Congress to vote it into being. The Federal Reserve Act helped establish the central privatized bank of the US, the Federal Reserve. This bank controls our money supply, value of the US dollar, and interest rates within the US.

NEW DEAL & SOCIAL SECURITY

   Much of Franklin Delano Roosevelt's New Deal, mainly
social security, was modeled after Bismarck's State
Pension Plan from 1880's in the German Empire. Bismarck
implemented that plan to dissuade and discourage the rise
of socialism in their country. He did that to make the
German populace feel that they didn't have to rely on such
a movement to get what they want and that they could rely
on their government to make smart tactical decisions in
their best interests to help promote both them and the
economy. He also did it to help the disenfranchised
mentally and physically handicapped in the country.
   People often criticize Social Security to be theft since our
taxes help fund it. That's not the case though. It is not theft.
It is a tool and agency that helps to provide money for the
elderly and disabled within our country, who have made
prolonged contributions within the workforce as well as
helped to preserve the American way. The elderly are
entitled and deserve a portion of the money of which our

government taxes from us. It is a way of giving back to them and honoring them for their contributions in society.

MARIJUANA LEGALIZATION

The idea of the federal legalization of marijuana is something that has not entirely been new within the past twenty four years. Its been floating around for many years before the turn of the 20th century to the 21st. I, for one, am in full support of its legalization. It should be done so purely from a medicinal and various product based corner. It can be used as an inexpensive raw and easily renewable material to produce plastics, textiles, oils, paper, rope, and medicines to help combat cancer, various forms of ADHD, and anxiety.

Fully legalizing weed within the US would also hit the income of the various Cartels and criminal underworld organizations within our borders. That reduction of their income could force them to cease some of their illegal operations as well as reduce some corruption. Recreational usage is fine, but should be regulated like alcohol with age restrictions, not having their distribution facilities be near schools, and have their profit incomes be taxed. The taxes imposed upon the distribution of weed should vary from state to state, depending upon population, cost of living within those regions, and other factors.

Marijuana is federally illegal in the first place due to the American civil servant Harry J. Anslinger's efforts throughout the 1920's-1960's. He helped spearhead the Federal Bureau of Narcotics, which was the predecessor to the Drug Enforcement Agency, under the Treasury Department. That, and news journalist, business tycoon William Randolph Hearst's efforts to have it illegalized since weed was, and still is, considered an inexpensive and renewable material in the manufacture of paper. Marijuana would have crippled his timber industry investments.

RELIGIOUS POLICY

In the regards to the possibility of religious taxation within the US, I personally feel that it should not entirely be tax exempt. That feeling only goes towards the sham religions, like Mormonism and Scientology. Those two religions were started by scam artists in the first place. The Abrahamic religions and religions from the East such as Taoism, Buddhism, Hindu, Confucianism, and the various forms of oriental religions should be respected and kept within the realms of tax exempt. Above all the ideas of our ancestors and Founding Fathers with the separation of church & state should be respected and honored.

Mormonism had Joseph Smith start their religion with being their first and central prophet, but he scammed numerous people before he even started the religion and even during it. Have you actually even heard the story of how Mormonism started in the first place? It's absolutely absurd. Magical seeing stones of which he uses to read off of gold plates that he dug up in the wilderness after an angel told him where to find them. Those stones and plates couldn't be seen and read by anyone but him, and having to read them out of a hat to a single publicist and businessman. Jesus supposedly being in America and the Native Americans being originally white until they displeased God, who turned their skin red. It's all absurd and can be disproven with both actual history and science.

Scientology was started by L. Ron Hubbard, a science fiction writer for Christ's sake. Almost everything that Scientologists believe can be disproven and are even more outlandish and absurd than Mormonism. Numerous celebrities believe in it or have fallen out of it, feeling disillusioned by the principles and doctrines of the Church of Scientology. They just profit off people's desire to ask questions and yearning to know where we come from, what's our purpose in life, and why are we on this planet. They offer no real solutions and constantly make people pay out of their pocket to rise up through the podium ranks of their religion. Despite the fact they claim they're not a religion, they most certainly are, but a sham one that operates as a business at best that profits off of people much rather than offering them true knowledge and hope of a better tomorrow.

www.ingramcontent.com/pod-product-compliance
Lightning Source LLC
Chambersburg PA
CBHW050528290526
45786CB00007B/2737